A POSTCARD
FROM PAUL

A POSTCARD FROM PAUL

❧ THE LETTER OF PAUL TO PHILEMON ❧

BY

TIMOTHY J. E. CROSS

AMBASSADOR

Belfast Northern Ireland **Greenville** South Carolina

A Postcard from Paul
© Copyright 1999 Timothy Cross

ISBN 1 84030 050 7

Ambassador Publications
a division of
Ambassador Productions Ltd.
Providence House
16 Hillview Avenue,
Belfast, BT5 6JR
Northern Ireland

Emerald House
1 Chick Springs Road, Suite 203
Greenville,
South Carolina 29609, USA
www.emeraldhouse.com

CONTENTS

FOREWORD

IT IS MY GREAT PLEASURE TO COMMEND TO YOU
MY BROTHER AND FELLOW SERVANT IN THE LORD,
A Postcard From Paul for your careful and prayerful consid-
eration. Paul's brief letter to Philemon is surely one of the
neglected legacies of the Holy Spirit to the Christian Church.
After over fifty years of walking with Christ, I have to confess
that the number of times I have heard this charming and vital
letter expounded have been very rare indeed. Timothy Cross's
labour of love will go some way towards putting this right, by
bringing this short, largely unknown epistle alive for us today.
Having read through the manuscript at an early stage, I can
vouch for its agreeable blend of clear explanation, contemp-
orary application and Christ-centred devotion.

Although set in the first century, the message of Philemon is timeless. The Word of God is always relevant. G. Campbell Morgan used to say that Philemon is a 'picture of Christianity in its outworking.' Without further ado then *Tolle lege!* Take it and read it! In doing so, it is both my sincere prayer and the prayer of the author that precious souls will be edified, puzzled minds clarified, and the peerless Saviour glorified.

Joe Wilson MBE
Barry, S. Wales

INTRODUCTION

THE LURE OF THE 'BIG CITY' HAS PROVED TO BE A TEMPTATION FAR TOO STRONG FOR MANY YOUNG men. Such was certainly the case with one Onesimus in the first century. Onesimus was the slave of Philemon, a man of some wealth and a Christian believer. When Onesimus's 'itchy feet' got the better of him, he robbed his master of some money and fled to the city of Rome, seeking excitement amidst the anonymity of that crowded and thriving metropolis, the centre of the then known world.

Whilst in Rome however, Onesimus's life took a drastic and unexpected turn. In the providence of God he came under the influence of the apostle Paul, and through meeting Paul, he came under the irresistible influence of the Lord Jesus Christ, and was soundly converted to the Christian Faith.

Conversion to Christ is the most wonderful experience this side of eternity. 'Oh happy day when Jesus washed my sins away!' This apart, Onesimus's problems and dilemmas did not disappear instantly. There were complications from the fact that the apostle Paul – his father in the faith – was also a good friend of Philemon, Onesimus's aggrieved master. Although Paul would have been pleased to enjoy Onesimus's useful company in Rome, he considered it only right that Onesimus should return to the master he had wronged. At this, Onesimus understandably had grave doubts and fears, as in the first century a runaway slave would have been branded with an 'F' – *Fugitivus* . The law even permitted a master to execute a rebellious slave.

With the above considerations in mind, Paul wrote a 'covering letter' for Onesimus to take back to Philemon, his estranged master in Colossae, and this short epistle to Philemon is the result. The epistle to Philemon was a little note from Paul to Philemon exhorting him to receive back and welcome his runaway slave, now *a slave but more than a slave, . . . a beloved brother* (v. 16). Paul was the earthly bridge between the two estranged parties, just as the Gospel was the eternal bridge between the two. *Receive him as you would receive me* (v. 17), wrote Paul.

The name 'Philemon' means 'affectionate', and Paul's letter to Philemon certainly is this, as well as being a model of tact, diplomacy and politeness. It is probably the most personal of all Paul's letters in the New Testament, and in it the great apostle really lays bare his heart and humanity.

Although the letter to Philemon began life as a personal letter, it is now part of the incomparable Volume that constitutes the infallible Word of God! As we consider this small portion of God's Word then, be prepared to be blessed. You have no doubt heard of the story of the 'Prodigal Son', (see Luke 15), but you are now going to meet the 'Prodigal Slave'. You will surely meet yourself in the process. Martin Luther once said 'All of us are Onesimuses', and he was right. By nature, we are rebels and runaways from God Himself, just like our first ancestors in Eden. Behind the letter to Philemon then is a beautiful, real life illustration of the Gospel of reconciliation.

The Gospel is the Good News that *God was in Christ reconciling the world to Himself, not counting their trespasses against them* (2 Corinthians 5:19). To reconcile means 'to bring together two parties that are at odds.' In dealing with our sin on Calvary's cross, Christ dealt with the enmity which separates us from our Master and Maker. When we put our faith in Christ, God receives us into His family so that we, mere creatures though we are, may enjoy the friendship and fellowship with our Creator for both time and eternity.

The epistle to Philemon consists of only three hundred words in the original text. I have thus entitled our study using the anachronism *A Postcard from Paul* – just as I previously entitled a study of John's short second and third letters *Some Postcards from John.* A big and sincere 'thank you' to those who agreed to read through the manuscript, made valuable comments and suggestions and encouraged me to persevere in both my writing and my Christian walk.

Timothy J. E. Cross
Barry, South Wales

THE LETTER OF PAUL
TO PHILEMON

Paul, a prisoner for Christ Jesus, and Timothy our brother,

To Philemon our beloved fellow worker and Apphia our sister and Archippus our fellow soldier, and the church in your house:

Grace to you and peace from God our Father and the Lord Jesus Christ.

I thank my God always when I remember you in my prayers, because I hear of your love and of the faith which you have toward the Lord Jesus and all the saints, and I pray that the sharing of your faith may promote the knowledge of all the good that is ours in Christ. For I have derived much comfort from your love, my brother, because the hearts of the saints have been refreshed through you.

Accordingly, though I am bold enough in Christ to command you to do what is required, yet for love's sake I prefer to appeal to you – I, Paul, an ambassador and now a prisoner also for Christ Jesus – I appeal to you for my child, Onesimus, whose father I have become in my imprisonment. (Formerly he was useless to you, but now he is indeed useful to you and to me.) I am sending him back to you, sending my very heart. I would have been glad to keep him with me, in order that he might serve me on your behalf during my imprisonment for the gospel; but I preferred to do nothing without your consent in order that your goodness might not be by compulsion but of your own free will.

Perhaps this is why he was parted from you for a while, that you might have him back for ever, no longer as a slave but more than a slave, as a beloved brother, especially to me but how much more to you, both in the flesh and in the Lord. So if you consider me your partner, receive him as you would receive me. If he has wronged you at all, or owes you anything, charge that to my account. I, Paul, write this with my own hand, I will repay it – to say nothing of your owing me even your own self. Yes, brother, I want some benefit from you in the Lord. Refresh my heart in Christ.

Confident of your obedience, I write to you, knowing that you will do even more than I say. At the same time, prepare a guest room for me, for I am hoping through your prayers to be granted to you.

Epaphras, my fellow prisoner in Christ Jesus, sends greetings to you, and so do Mark, Aristarchus, Demas, and Luke, my fellow workers.

The grace of the Lord Jesus Christ be with your spirit.

one

THE PRISONER

Paul, a prisoner for Christ Jesus . . . (v.1)

IF WE ARE SITTING IN A COMFORTABLE ARMCHAIR
AS WE READ PAUL'S LETTERS TO THE EPHESIANS,
Philippians and Colossians, as well as this little letter to
Philemon, we may be inclined to forget that all of these letters
were written originally in conditions none too pleasant. They
were all written from a prison cell in Rome. Paul, however,
does not begin this letter with 'Paul, a prisoner of the Roman
State' but *Paul, a prisoner for Christ Jesus.* Paul then was
able to look beyond all the so called 'secondary causes'
and see that the ultimate cause of absolutely everything is the
sovereign will of God.

The *Shorter Catechism* reminds us in Q.7 that 'The decrees of God are His eternal purpose, according to the counsel of His will, whereby, for His own glory He hath fore-ordained whatsoever comes to pass.' In opening this letter so, Paul reveals his Christian maturity. He accepted the 'whatsoever.' Humanly speaking, he had every reason to complain about his harsh circumstances, but instead he submitted to the sovereign will of God.

We too can often feel imprisoned, but imprisoned in a less tangible way – imprisoned by circumstances, difficulties and physical and psychological handicaps. Can we, though, take everything that happens to us as coming from the hand of God, even when 'God moves in a mysterious way, His wonders to perform'? *My times are in Thy hand* (Psalm 31:15), confessed David to God, and so may we. This knowledge of God's sovereign control of all things is of especial comfort to us in our times of distress and adversity. It has been well said: 'Those who see the hand of God in everything can leave everything in the hand of God.'

The fact that Paul enjoyed communion with His Saviour even amidst the unpromising conditions of a prison cell, proves that Paul could 'walk the walk' as well as 'talk the talk.' In Philippians 4:11 ff. he wrote: *Not that I complain of want; for I have learned, in whatever state I am, to be content. I know how to be abased, and I know how to abound; in any and all circumstances I have learned the secret of facing plenty and hunger, abundance and want. I can do all things in Him who strengthens me.* When the jailor at Philippi heard those words he would have exclaimed 'Amen! Paul means what he says.' Whilst in his unconverted state, this Philippian jailor had treated Paul and his companion Silas most cruelly, and *put them into the inner prison and fastened their feet in the stocks* (Acts 16:24). The story though continues in a remarkable way, inexplicable apart from Divine grace, for *about midnight Paul and*

*Silas were praying and singing hymns to God, and the prison-
ers were listening to them* (Acts 16:25). There again is Paul's
contentment whatever his circumstances.

When Paul wrote to Philemon then, it was a case of
being *I, Paul . . . a prisoner also for Christ Jesus* (v.9). When
we know something of the character of our God, surely we
would far rather be shut up in a dark prison cell *in* God's will,
than be free in the daylight *out* of it. From the perspective of
eternity we will have cause to rejoice that we were once God's
prisoner rather than the Devil's free man.

two

ThE PersonneL

Paul . . . and Timothy our brother, . . .
To Philemon our beloved fellow worker and Apphia our sister and
Archippus our fellow soldier, and the church in your house
(vv.1,2).

WE ARE HERE INTRODUCED TO SOME OF THE MAIN 'DRAMATIS PERSONAE' OF PAUL'S LETTER TO Philemon, Onesimus excepted. Providence was kind to Paul in giving him the companionship of young Timothy in his prison cell. We can be sure that each were a source of mutual encouragement to the other, as they exhorted one other to persevere and keep trusting in God.

The letter of Paul to Philemon is primarily what it says –
a short letter from Paul to Philemon, a wealthy slave owner in
Colossae. Philemon however was a *Christian* slave owner,
whose hospitality was such that he put his home at the Lord's
disposal, opening his doors to all the Christians in the locality.
Every Sunday would see a fellowship of Christians gathering
in the Name of Jesus in Philemon's house for worship – prayer,
the Lord's Supper and the careful reading and exposition of
Holy Scripture.

In a secondary way, the letter to Philemon was also to
Apphia and *Archippus.* Commentators are generally agreed
that Apphia was Philemon's wife, (the Bible has much to say
about Christian marriage, founded on Christ Jesus.) More
speculatively though, it is suggested that Archippus was the
son of Philemon and Apphia, and that he had been entrusted
with some responsibility in running church affairs in the
absence of *Epaphras* (v. 24), whose faithful preaching (see
Colossians 1:7) had been instrumental in founding the church
at Colossae. That Archippus was now active in the Lord's
service fits Colossians 4:17 well: *And say to Archippus, 'See
that you fulfil the ministry which you have received in the Lord.'*

The terms used to describe all these people, both
individually and collectively, are most revealing. Let us look
at some of them:-

1. *Timothy our brother . . . Apphia our sister.*

Christians are all in the same family. The spiritual blood-
tie of Christians, i.e. the bond of being redeemed by the blood
of Christ, is stronger than even a natural blood-tie. It is said
that 'blood is thicker than water', and never is this more true
than in the family of God, a family which transcends race,
nationality and even time itself. Christians are brothers and

sisters who know God as their Father through Jesus Christ. 'Adoption' is a blessed Christian truth and reality, and one of the ways in which the Bible describes salvation. 'Adoption is an act of God's free grace whereby we are received into the number and have a right to all the privileges of the sons of God' (*Shorter Catechism* , Q. 34).

2. *Philemon our beloved fellow worker.*

There is a bond of family love between Christians which is better experienced than described. Philemon was beloved:-

> Blest be the tie that binds
> our hearts in Christian love,
> The fellowship of kindred minds
> is like to that above.

Philemon was also a 'fellow'. Biblical Christianity knows nothing of an isolated individualism. A solitary Christian is a contradiction and denial of the body of Christ.

Notice that Philemon has gone down in history as a *worker* and not a shirker, a labourer not a loafer. By this Paul means that Philemon was a worker for the kingdom of God, who testified to the Gospel in word and deed. *Working together with Him* (2 Corinthians 6:1), *For we are God's fellow workers* (1 Corinthians 3:9), reminding us that God still uses his earthly workers to accomplish His eternal purposes. We may not have Philemon's means at our disposal, but we too can be a 'fellow worker' if we consecrate who we are and what we have to God:-

> There's a work for Jesus
> Ready at your hand,

> 'Tis a task the Master
> Just for you has planned,
> Haste to do His bidding
> Yield Him service true,
> There's a work for Jesus
> None but you can do.

3. *Archippus our fellow soldier.*

The metaphor here changes to a military one. Christianity involves warfare as well as welfare. There is the fight of faith, which makes it more of a battleground than a playground. Paul reminded the Ephesians of the necessity of putting on the whole armour of God: *For we are not contending against flesh and blood but against the principalities, against the powers, against the world rulers of this present darkness, against the spiritual hosts of wickedness in the heavenly places* (Ephesians 6:12). Praying for another's salvation is actually engaging in spiritual warfare. Who would guess that one frail in body and lowly in this world, yet one who prays faithfully is actually one of the Lord's warriors? The Bible tells us so, *For though we live in the world, we are not carrying on a worldly war, for the weapons of our warfare are not worldly but have divine powers to destroy strongholds* (2 Corinthians 10:3,4). The hymnist got it right:-

> Stand up stand up for Jesus
> Ye soldiers of the cross
> Lift high His royal banner
> it must not suffer loss
> From victory unto victory
> His army shall He lead
> Till every foe is vanquished
> And Christ is Lord indeed.

4. *The church in your house.*

Here we move to a collective as opposed to a personal description. How many people will immediately think of a building when the word 'church' is mentioned? According to the New Testament though, the church is primarily a people and not a building – *living stones . . . built into a spiritual house* (1 Peter 2:5). What a contrast to lifeless bricks and mortar! Whilst many of us enjoy the facilities of a special 'church building', set apart exclusively for divine worship and the preaching of the Gospel, we should remind ourselves that no such special buildings were legal until the fourth century AD. This lack of 'consecrated buildings' though certainly did not hinder the spread of the Gospel.

In the New Testament then, 'church' refers to the believing Christian community - the gathering together of those saved by God's grace in Jesus Christ. They are a people whom God has chosen out of lost humanity to whom He makes the promise: 'I will be their God and they shall be my people.' The New Testament views the church as a multi-faceted diamond. What a people are the church! They are the elect, chosen in Christ *before the foundation of the world* (Ephesians 1:4). They are the people for whom Christ died to save (see Ephesians 1:7), and they are the ones to whom God, by His Holy Spirit, applies the finished work of Christ, making it effective in them, enabling them to appropriate all the blessings of salvation.

The church: God's redeemed, God's special people. These are the people who are to enjoy God's presence for all eternity!

three

THE PATTERN

*Grace to you and peace from God our Father and the
Lord Jesus Christ* (v.3).

EVERY ONE OF PAUL'S LETTERS OPENS WITH A SIMI-
LAR, BLESSED PATTERN AND FORMULA TO THIS ONE:
*Grace to you and peace from God the Father and the Lord
Jesus Christ.* It is almost as if it is Paul's signature tune! (See
Romans 1:7, 1 Corinthians 1:3, 2 Corinthians 1:2, Galatians
1:3, Ephesians 1:2, Philippians 1:2, Colossians 1:2). Notice in
passing the complete co-equality of God the Father and God
the Son in this formula. In putting *God the Father and the
Lord Jesus Christ* side-by-side like so, Paul betrays His belief
in the absolute deity of Christ.

Grace to you and peace.

This greeting combines both Greek and Hebrew ideas. The Greek *charis* refers to the unmerited favour and undeserved kindness of God to sinners. The Hebrew word *shalom* is an umbrella term for the blessing of God, holding such a meaning as peace, wholeness, spiritual prosperity and well-being. G. B. Wilson comments:- 'Grace is the unmerited favour of God which brings sinners to salvation in Christ, and peace is that state of spiritual well-being that flows from the reception of this grace.'

Paul, the converted Pharisee, could say with hand on heart *by the grace of God I am what I am* (1 Corinthians 15:10). So transformed by God's grace was Paul, that he viewed his whole life's work in terms of *if only I may accomplish my course and the ministry which I received from the Lord Jesus, to testify to the gospel of the grace of God* (Acts 20:24).

It is God's grace, and God's grace alone, which is the only lasting means of peace to the guilty sinner. It is God's grace in sending Jesus Christ to die for our sins which bestows *the peace of God which passes all understanding* (Philippians 4:7). This particular peace is a peace which the world can neither give nor take away (cf John 14:27). It is the peace of sins forgiven; it is the peace of being right with God; it is the peace of never needing to fear the judgment day; it is the peace of having a home in heaven, prepared for us by the Saviour who loves us.

The grace of God in the Gospel is the only lasting and eternal source of peace. Paul explained to Philemon's friends in Colossae something of the significance of the cross of Christ. It was there, wrote Paul, that the Lord Jesus was *making peace by the blood of His cross* (Colossians 1:20). Paul's experience was normal Christian experience: *Therefore, since we are justified by faith we have peace with God through our Lord Jesus Christ* (Romans 5:1).

The incomparable and eternal peace of being a recipient of God's grace!

I hear the words of love,
I gaze upon the blood.
I see the mighty sacrifice,
And I have peace with God

'Tis everlasting peace,
Sure as Jehovah's name.
'Tis stable as His steadfast throne,
For evermore the same.

four

THE PRAYERS

*Grace to you and peace from God our Father and the
Lord Jesus Christ* (v.3).

*I thank my God always when I remember you in my prayers,
because I hear of your love and of the faith which you have
toward the Lord Jesus and all the saints , and I pray that the
sharing of your faith may promote the knowledge of all the good
that is ours in Christ*
(vv. 4-6).

LIKE HIS MASTER, PAUL WAS A MAN OF PRAYER.
PAUL ENJOYED AN INTIMATE UNION AND COMMUN-
ion with God through this means, and here, he lets us in some-
what on his prayer life. In relation to Philemon his prayers
involved:-

1. Thanks for what Philemon had commenced doing and
2. Hopes for what Philemon will continue to be doing.

1. Paul prays with thanks for what Philemon had commenced doing.

Notice first of all how in his prayers Paul gives thanks to God for Philemon's faith and love. Perhaps we would have congratulated Philemon personally rather than giving thanks to God, so this comes a corrective reminder that Christian virtue is divinely rather than self originated:-

> Every virtue we possess and every victory won
> and every thought of holiness are His alone.

. . . your love and of the faith which you have toward the Lord Jesus and all the saints.

The Christian's love for Jesus is a reciprocal response to *the Son of God who loved me and gave Himself for me* (Galatians 2:20). *We love Him, because He first loved us* (1 John 4:19). As with love though, so with faith. Faith is a, if not *the* cardinal Christian virtue, as it is through our divinely wrought faith that salvation is received. 'Faith in Jesus Christ is a saving grace whereby we receive and rest upon Him alone for salvation as He is offered to us in the Gospel' (*Shorter Catechism*, Q.86). *Love and . . . faith* being *toward the Lord Jesus Christ* are thus the primary marks of a Christian, and divine in their object. This notwithstanding, *love and . . . faith* both are, and are to be reflected *toward . . . all the saints* as well.

Love and faith do not, and cannot exist in a spiritual vacuum, but have, and should have an earthly reflection and overflow in the Christian community, the church. If either an individual Christian or a corporate Christian community is not characterised by a degree of mutual love and faithfulness towards each other – allowances being made for the indwelling sin which will always plague us this side of eternity – we may have just cause to doubt whether a genuine work of God has been wrought. Our 'vertical' relationship with God in heaven above can only have a 'horizontal' outcome here on earth below. The life of heaven can only effect our life on earth. The Bible is blunt: *If any one says 'I love God' and hates his brother, he is a liar; for he who does not love his brother whom he has seen, cannot love God whom he has not seen. And this commandment we have from Him, that he who loves God should love his brother also* (1 John 4:20,21).

2. Paul prays with hopes for what Philemon will continue to be doing.

. . . and I pray that the sharing of your faith may promote the knowledge of all the good that is ours in Christ

To share our faith is to share the blessings and benefits of our faith – *the good that is ours in Christ.* 'To know Christ is to know his benefits', as Luther said. How do we begin to enumerate the good that really is ours in Christ? We will have an eternity to do so and we will need it! In Ephesians Paul mentioned *the unsearchable riches of Christ* (Ephesians 3:8) and went on to say that, in one sense, *the love of Christ* , being so great *surpasses knowledge* (Ephesians 3:19). Theologians though have most helpfully attempted to make some sort of categorisation of *the good that is ours in Christ.* Categorising a blessing, of course, is not the same as experiencing the blessing, but how valuable is the *Shorter Catechism* in the following enumerations. They are not exhaustive, but they make us count our many blessings:-

Q. 32: What benefits do they that are effectually called partake of in this life?

A: They that are effectually called do in this life partake of justification, adoption and sanctification, and the several benefits which in this life do either accompany or flow from them.

Q. 33: What is justification?

A: Justification is an act of God's free grace, wherein He pardoneth all our sins and accepteth us as righteous in His sight, only for the righteousness of Christ imputed to us, and received by faith alone.

Q. 34: What is adoption?

A. Adoption is an act of God's free grace, whereby we are received into the number and have a right to all the privileges of the sons of God.

Q. 35: What is sanctification?

A: Sanctification is the work of God's free grace, whereby we are renewed in the whole man after the image of God, and are enabled more and more to die unto sin and live unto righteousness.

Q. 36: What are the benefits which in this life do accompany or flow from justification, adoption and sanctification?

A: The benefits which in this life do accompany or flow from justification, adoption and sanctification are, assurance of God's love, peace of conscience, joy in the Holy Ghost, increase of grace, and perseverance therein to the end.

Q. 37: What benefits do believers receive from Christ at death?

A: The souls of believers are at their death made perfect in holiness and do immediately pass into glory; and their bodies, being still united to Christ, do rest in their graves till the resurrection.

Q. 38: What benefits do believers receive from Christ at the resurrection?

A. At the resurrection, believers being raised up in glory, shall be openly acknowledged and acquitted in the day of judgment, and made perfectly blessed in the full enjoying of God to all eternity.

The good which is ours in Christ? Very much so. This being so, the sharing of our faith is surely the kindest act we can ever perform.

five

ThE PleasurE

For I have derived much joy and comfort from your love,
my brother, because the hearts of the saints have been
refreshed through you (v.7).

PAUL'S THOUGHTS OF PHILEMON WERE MOST
PLEASANT. KNOWING OF PHILEMON'S EVIDENT AND
manifest Christian love was a source of much joy and comfort
to the aged apostle. Philemon's love though was no mere
emotion but highly practical: *the hearts of the saints have been*
refreshed through you. Interestingly, this word *refreshed* is
the same one used in the Saviour's promise *I will give you rest*
(Matthew 11:28). Philemon then, in a lesser way than his
Master, was a source of refreshment, rest and relief to his

fellow believers. 'No doubt Philemon had used his wealth to minister to the needs of his fellow believers in some time of crises, and this may have ben in connection with the great earthquake of AD 60' (G. B. Wilson).

We saw in verse 2 that Philemon's home was an 'open house' for Christians, and how many of us since the first century have cause to thank God for Christian 'open homes' – Christian homes which have been a source of refreshment, refuge, renewal and solace from all the battles and trials of life. Such sanctuaries, although perhaps poor in this world's goods, remind us of 'The Palace Beautiful' in Bunyan's *Pilgrim's Progress* :-

> '. . . there was a very stately palace before him, the name of which was Beautiful . . .
> 'So I saw in my dream, that he made haste, and went forward, that if possible he might get lodging there.
> 'Then said Christian to the Porter, 'Sir, what house is this? And may I lodge here tonight?' The Porter answered, 'This house was built by the Lord of the hill, and He built it for the relief and security of Pilgrims."

Such was Philemon's home – a 'Palace Beautiful' – and such have been many Christian homes since – places of relief and security. Places where *the hearts of the saints have been refreshed.*

six

ThE PurposE

*Accordingly, though I am bold enough in Christ to command
you to do what is required, yet for love's sake – I, Paul, an
ambassador and now a prisoner also for Christ Jesus – I appeal
to you for my child Onesimus, whose father I have become in my
imprisonment. (Formerly he was useless to you, but now he is
indeed useful to you and to me.) I am sending him back to you,
sending my very heart. I would have been glad to keep him with
me, in order that he might serve me on your behalf during
my imprisonment for the Gospel; but I preferred to do nothing
without your consent in order that your goodness might not be
by compulsion but of your own free will.*

*Perhaps this is why he was parted from you for a while,
that you might have him back for ever, no longer as a slave but
more than a slave, as a beloved brother, especially to me but how
much more to you, both in the flesh and in the Lord. So if you
consider me your partner, receive him as you would receive me*
(vv.8-17).

1. The Grand Reconciliation.

With this lengthy section we are taken to the heart of the letter to Philemon. Here, Paul gets 'to the point', and reveals his main purpose in writing which may be summarised as follows:-

Paul wrote to Philemon with a gentle, tactful and persuasive plea for him to receive his runaway slave Onesimus back. Paul's plea is based on the fact that Philemon has good cause to welcome Onesimus as the latter is now a fellow Christian believer.

Here then we have the clue verses to this little letter:- *I appeal to you for my child, Onesimus* (v.10) . . . *receive him as you would receive me* (v.17).

Underlying and undergirding this, albeit implicitly, is the Gospel of reconciliation. We can almost hear the Lord Jesus Christ interceding for His 'runaways' just as Paul interceded for Onesimus. Jesus intercedes for His own. *He ever lives to make intercession for them* (Hebrews 7:25). *We have an advocate with the Father, Jesus Christ the righteous* (1 John 2:1). Jesus now, as it were, says to the Father 'Receive them as you receive me.' It is a glorious Gospel truth that every Christian is received and accepted by God because of the merits and mediation of the Lord Jesus Christ.

The epistle to Philemon then is a letter which reveals the practical outworking of the Gospel of reconciliation. In it, we see parties which are brought together in a manner which is inexplicable apart from divine grace: We see Paul, the Jew and educated Pharisee, brought together with Onesimus, an uneducated Gentile and runaway slave – and slaves were very near to the bottom rung of the social scale. Also, of course, in the main thrust of the letter, we see Onesimus reconciled to his master Philemon, for as Paul wrote to Onesimus's church to be, in the Gospel *Here there cannot be Greek and J:*

*circumcised and uncircumcised, ... slave, free man, but Christ
is all, and in all* (Colossians 3:11, cf Galatians 3:28).

2. The Good Reasons.

But why should Philemon receive Onesimus, his runaway slave? Wasn't it normal and logical to either brand him
with an 'F' – Fugative! – or even to execute him as a bad lot?
Such would be the normal course of action in Biblical days.
But with Onesimus and Philemon the logical had been over-
rided by the Theological! God had intervened! An enormous
change had occurred. Paul's persuasive reasoning is quite
irresistible:-

i. Onesimus was now a Christian man.

*I appeal to you for my child, Onesimus, whose father I
have become in my imprisonment* (v.10). Such seems to be the
way in which Paul refers to his spiritual offspring – those whom
he had been instrumental in leading to faith in Christ. Paul
wrote to the Corinthians *I became your father in Christ Jesus
through the Gospel* (1 Corinthians 4:15). Compare also 2 Timothy 1:2: *Timothy, my beloved child.*
Onesimus then was not the Onesimus Philemon had
known previously! The Bible is clear: *If any one is in Christ,
he is a new creation; the old has passed away, behold, the new
has come* (2 Corinthians 5:17). Onesimus's conversion brought
him into a new standing before both God and God's people,
and Paul exhorted Philemon to take this into account: *have
him back for ever, no longer as a slave but more than a slave,
as a beloved brother, especially to me but how much more to
you* (vv.15,16).
How astounding, astonishing and amazing. Onesimus's
material status was that of a mere slave, the lowest of the low.

Yet Onesimus's spiritual status was that of a child of God, the highest of the high! H. A. W. Meyer puts it very aptly: 'In the flesh Philemon had the brother for a slave; in the Lord he had the slave for a brother.'

Now then, as a child of God, Onesimus – like Philemon – knew what it was to be adopted by grace into the family of God. Philemon and Onesimus were now brothers in the Lord! They now had the same Father, God the Father; they had both been redeemed by the same Saviour's precious blood; they were both indwelt by the same Holy Spirit. It would be just unthinkable and inconceivable that Philemon would turn away such a person. When we hurt a member of our own family the hurt rebounds back on ourselves.

ii. Onesimus was now a changed man.

As a Christian man, Onesimus was now a changed and transformed man. *Formerly he was useless (achreston) to you, but now he is indeed useful (euchreston) to you and to me* (v.11).

Paul convinces Philemon that Onesimus has been reformed and transformed. In Colossians 4:9 Paul describes Onesimus as:*Onesimus, the faithful and beloved brother.* The name 'Onesimus' means 'useful' or 'profitable', so with a touch of humour, Paul tells Philemon that Onesimus is finally living up to his useful name. (A similar humour is evident in verse 20: *I want some benefit from you in the Lord.* Here Paul puns and plays on the word 'benefit'. A literal translation would read 'I want some onaimen from you in the Lord.')

iii. Onesimus was now a charged man.

Paul was confident that Onesimus's conversion was genuine and not phoney, as Onesimus had already proved his worth. *he is indeed useful to you and to me* (v.11), *I would have been glad to keep him with me, in order that he might serve me on your behalf during my imprisonment for the Gospel* (v.13).

A fruit of genuine conversion is that of a purposeful, useful and fruitful life. *He redeems your life from the pit* (Psalm 103:4, which could also be rendered 'He redeems your life from waste.') Whilst we are most definitely saved by faith and not by works, true faith definitely works! *For we are His workmanship, created in Christ Jesus for good works, which God prepared beforehand, that we should walk in them* (Ephesians 2:10). True Christian good works are not a matter of slavish obedience, but motivated from a heart of gratitude for benefits and blessings received. In Colossians 3:22 Paul wrote to Onesimus's fellow slaves at Colossae: *Slaves, obey in everything those who are your earthly masters, not with eye service as men-pleasers, but in singleness of heart, fearing the Lord –* and Paul had every evidence and confidence that Onesimus's life did and would manifest such singleness of heart and God-fearing service. And so Paul sent Onesimus back home to his master. Paul's words in 1 Timothy 6:1-2 seem to be relevant here: *Let all who are under the yoke of slavery regard their masters as worthy of all honour, so that the name of God and the teaching may not be defamed. Those who have believing masters must not be disrespectful on the ground that they are brethren; rather they must serve all the better since those who benefit by their service are believers and beloved.*

'What a wonderful change in my life has been brought, since Jesus came into my heart', goes one hymn. Onesimus would have sung it out loud, with warmth and sincerity. Conversion makes us children of God. Conversion reconciles us to our Maker and to His people. Conversion changes our direction. Conversion enables us to live a fruitful life. Conversion motivates us to want to live a life that is pleasing to God.

seven

ThE ProvidencE

Perhaps this was why he was parted from you for a while, that you might have him back forever, no longer as a slave but more than a slave, as a beloved brother . . . (vv.15,16).

PERHAPS THIS WAS WHY HE WAS PARTED FROM YOU ... In this verse we glimpse something of the mystery of Providence at work. Surely we would have said that Onesimus absconded from Philemon. Paul however suggests that while Onesimus was fully responsible for his actions, it was yet God Himself who caused Onesimus to flee from his master. . . .*he was parted from you for a while* . What a mystery. All is fore-ordained and yet free will is given. Whilst we are unable to reconcile God's sovereignty with human free will, we are forced to confess that God Himself can.

The story of Onesimus and Philemon is a beautiful, real-life illustration of Romans 8:28: *We know that in everything God works for good with those who love Him, who are called according to His purpose.* Would Philemon really have believed that God was working for his good when Onesimus had just robbed him and deserted him? Hardly. But unknown to Philemon, God was in complete control. He rules and over-rules. Onesimus's desertion to Rome had actually been foreordained by God. Onesimus was one of God's elect – however unlikely this seemed initially – and God had foreordained that the means to his salvation would be hearing the words of life from the lips of the apostle Paul in the Roman capital. In hearing and believing Onesimus was saved! In being saved he was now more *than a slave . . . a beloved brother* to both Paul and Philemon. In cutting his earthly ties Onesimus had inadvertantly caused eternal ties to be formed! *that you might have him back forever* reminding us that Christians are to spend eternity together – a blessed eternity occupied by worshipping God.

God's providence. It is certainly seen in the salvation of Onesimus, in all its simplicity and in all its intricacy. The God who has ordained salvation for His elect through the death of Christ has also ordained the means to that salvation. In Onesimus's case it involved a visit to a Roman prison cell far away from his home. Truly, *those whom He predestined He also called; and those whom He called He also justified; and those whom He justified He also glorified* (Romans 8:30).

Philemon then, in hearing of Onesimus's conversion, would be able to look back and see that God had brought him blessing and joy out of seemingly harsh providences:-

> Ill that He blesses is our good
> and unblessed good is ill

> But all is right that seems so wrong
> if it be His sweet will.

Philemon may have been reminded of the life of Joseph. God brought blessing out of harsh circumstances and even human wickedness here also. Philemon could even have quoted to Onesimus the very words that Joseph eventually said to his brothers: *Fear not, for am I in the place of God? As for you, you meant evil against me; but God meant it for good . . .* (Genesis 50:19,20).

Onesimus's realationship with Philemon had been transformed by God. No longer was it now a case of a legalistic, drudging duty. The bondsman was now the brother. Eternity could not break the internal, spiritual tie that had been formed. They were now blood brothers! Both owed their salvation to the blood of Jesus. How God over-rules the sinful actions of men!

By way of application, try and put yourself in Philemon's shoes and ask yourself the question 'How do I cope and react when harsh providence comes my way?' Life can be full of getting what we do not want and not getting what we do want. Can we trust God on such occasions and in such circumstances? Chapter III of the *Westminster Confession of Faith* is so relevant to us here:-

> God, from all eternity, did, by the most wise and holy counsel of His own will, freely, and unchangeably ordain whatsoever comes to pass: yet so, as thereby neither is God the author of sin, nor is violence offered to the will of the creatures; nor is the liberty or contingency of second causes taken away, but rather established.

Trials reveal the true calibre of our faith. They reveal

whether we really believe that *in everything God works for good with those who love Him* (Romans 8:28). Oh to be like Job! He was sorely tried but could yet confess: *But He knows the way that I take; when He has tried me I shall come forth as gold* (Job 23:10).

eight

THE PLEDGE

If he has wronged you at all, or owes you anything, charge
that to my account. I, Paul, write this with my own hand, I will
repay it . . . (vv.18,19).

IN ORDER TO BE ABLE TO 'EMIGRATE' FROM
COLOSSAE TO ROME, ONESIMUS, A POOR, PENNILESS
slave, would have needed money. At the time he was not
a Christian and so had no fear of God and no respect and
reverence for God's law. He thus had no qualms at all about
breaking the eighth commandment and robbing his master. He
literally took the money and ran. Now, however, as a saved
man, he was fully repentant for his actions. This apart though,

his action could not be undone. It still stood as an obstacle against Onesimus's reconciliation to his master Philemon. At this point therefore Paul stepped in and made a pledge. Paul promised Philemon that he would take personal responsibility for any debts that Onesimus owed him. If he . . . *owes you anything, charge that to my account . . . I will repay it.* Paul was so serious that he even took the pen away from the amaneuensis to whom he was dictating the letter and made a pledge to repay – an IOU – in his own handwriting. Paul was thus Onesimus's guarantor. The document now bound him to be so.

In our introduction we intimated that underlying and undergirding the letter to Philemon is the Gospel of reconciliation. Never is this more so than now, in Paul's pledge to write off all of Onesimus's debts. *Charge that to my account . . . I will repay . . .*

The Gospel of reconciliation is all about the forgiveness of sins through Christ's paying the ultimate cost on our behalf. Forgiveness actually means 'remission', i.e. the cancellation of all our debt against God. Ephesians 1:7: *In Him we have redemption through His blood, the forgiveness of our trespasses according to the riches of His grace.* 1 John 2:12: *I am writing to you little children because your sins are forgiven for His sake.*

As Onesimus's remission rested on the intervening work of Paul, so likewise the Christian's remission – the cancellation of the debt of our sin – rests on the intervening, atoning work of Christ. Paul reminded the Colossians of Christ: *having forgiven us all our trespasses, having cancelled the bond (IOU) which stood against us with its legal demands. This He laid aside, nailing it to the cross* (Colossians 2:13,14). The forgiveness of sins through the paying of a price – the price of Christ's blood – just about summarises what the Gospel is all about.

Charge that to my account . . . promises Paul. It leads us to the heart of the Gospel. Paradoxically, forgiveness is both absolutely free and yet immensely costly. Forgiveness occurs because our sins were charged to Christ's account, and He paid the price and cancelled out our debt. 2 Corinthians 5:21 must be one of the most wonderful and profoundest verses in the Bible. It brings us to the doctrine of imputation. Our sins were imputed to Christ – charged to His account. Likewise, because of Calvary, Christ's righteousness is credited to our account, putting us 'in the black' with Almighty God. Read 2 Corinthians 5:21 slowly, and ponder the great transaction that occured at Calvary: *For our sake He made Him to be sin who knew no sin, so that in Him we might become the righteousness of God.*

Paul then pledged Onesimus's earthly welfare. If we are Christ's though, we know that He has pledged our eternal welfare! On Calvary He wrote off the debt of our sin. The transaction of Calvary is such that our 'balance' with God is restored as soon as we cast ourselves on Christ for mercy.

What a paradox is Calvary! What a paradox is salvation! It is free but costly. It means great riches for bankrupt debtors. It involved the sinless One being reckoned sinful in God's sight, so that sinners may be reckoned righteous. Eternity will surely be too short to plumb its depths and sing our great Redeemer's praise.

'All of us are Onesimus's' said Martin Luther. And so we are, if we belong to Christ. He has written off all our debts against God.

> What mighty sum paid all my debt
> When I a bondman stood
> And has my soul at freedom set
> Tis Jesus' precious blood

Jesus paid it all
All to Him I owe
Sin had left its crimson stain
He washed it white as snow.

ThE PERSUASIoN

. . . to say nothing of your owing me even your own self. Yes,
brother, I want some benefit (onaimen) from you in the Lord
(vv.19b, 20).

STILL CENTRAL TO THE EPISTLE'S PURPOSE, PAUL
HERE, EMPLOYING GENTLE PERSUASION, REMINDS
Philemon that, whilst he is seeking a favour from him, he,
Philemon, actually is in debt to the greater favour already
showed to him by Paul, for it was Paul who had lead Philemon
to Christ. Philemon then, humanly speaking, owed his own
soul to Paul. Philemon's debt to Paul was thus incalculable. So
how could he refuse Paul's request and not show favour to
Onesimus?

'By putting it this way, Paul wishes to remind Philemon of the pardon he himself received, to make him understand how grace freely received calls to remission of debt, when a fellow sinner also comes to conversion' (C. Bouma, cited by Muller in G. B. Wilson).

In Matthew 10:8 Jesus tells His disciples *Freely ye have received, freely give* (KJV). Bearing the case of Paul, Philemon and Onesimus in mind though, it is also Scriptural to teach 'Freely you have been forgiven, freely forgive.' Paul wrote to Philemon's church at Colossae: *as the Lord has forgiven you, so you must also forgive* (Colossians 3:13, cf Ephesians 4:32). In Matthew 18:23-35 the Lord Jesus Christ Himself told the 'Parable of the Unjust Servant'. Forgiveness – the literal cancellation of debt – is central to this parable. In it a master freely forgives his servant's financial debt, and was most distressed when he found that this servant then refused to forgive a fellow servant for his lesser debt: '*You wicked servant! I forgave you all that debt because you besought me; and should not you have had mercy on your fellow servant, as I had mercy on you?*

On the human level, forgiveness can be so very difficult. Many of us have been deeply wounded by something which someone has done to us in the past. It is even more complicated if we have been hurt by a fellow believer. What can we do? All we can do is to meditate on Calvary and God's free forgiveness for our sins wrought there. When we are honest with ourselves, we know the incalculable debt in which we are to God, due to who we are and what we have done; but we know also that God has forgiven us for Jesus' sake. Having received His infinite and eternal forgiveness, how can we then bear grudges against our fellows? The true Christian ethic flows from forgiveness received. We forgive because we have been forgiven. Grace leads to gratitude which leads to showing grace.

Onesimus was in debt to Philemon. Philemon was in debt to God. God had written off all Philemon's debts. Philemon was to write off all Onesimus's. The Lord Jesus Christ taught us to pray: *And forgive us our debts, as we also have forgiven our debtors* (Matthew 6:12).

ten

THE PREACHING

Onesimus, whose father I have become in my imprisonment (v.10)
. . . to say nothing of your owing me even your own self (v.19).

TAKING AN IMPORTANT DIVERSION, AND PUTTING
THE ABOVE VERSES SIDE-BY-SIDE, WE SEE THAT
Paul was the spiritual father of both Onesimus and Philemon.

Onesimus had been lead to Christ by Paul in a Roman
prison cell. Luke ends the book of Acts with Paul in prison in
Rome, and records how *he welcomed all who came to him,*
preaching the kingdom of God and teaching about the Lord
Jesus Christ quite openly and unhindered (Acts 28:30,31).

Philemon had also been led to Christ by Paul, but when and how, Scripture is silent. Paul had never actually visited Colossae, Philemon's home (see Colossians 2:1) and it was Epaphras who had been the human instrument in founding the church there. But under the providence of God, Philemon had had cause to leave Colossae for a while, and coming under the influence of Paul he came under the influence of Christ. We must not speculate when Scripture is silent, but in Acts 19:10 we read of Paul's mission in Ephesus that *all the residents of Asia heard the Word of the Lord.* Maybe Philemon was in Ephesus at that time on business? Perhaps it was then that he heard the words of eternal life.

Whilst the details of both Onesimus's and Philemon's conversions are unclear, we can be clear when we state that *preaching* was the means to their conversion. Preaching involves the verbal communication of God's truth, by God's chosen servant to meet God's chosen peoples' need. Paul was predominantly a preacher. He knew that it was through this means that God called sinners to Himself. Paul testified that *Christ did not send me to baptize but to preach the Gospel* (1 Corinthians 1:18) and that *it pleased God through the folly of what we preach to save those who believe* (1 Corinthians 1:21b). For Paul, preaching was both a duty and a burden which he had to discharge: *Woe to me if I do not preach the Gospel!* (1 Corinthians 9:16). *I am eager to preach the Gospel . . . For I am not ashamed of the Gospel; it is the power of God for salvation to everyone who has faith* (Romans 1:15,16). Paul knew that *faith comes from what is heard, and what is heard comes from the preaching of Christ* (Romans 10:17).

Onesimus, in Rome, heard Paul *preaching the kingdom of God* (Acts 28:31). Philemon's Asian countrymen *heard the Word of the Lord* (Acts 19:10). Such is the divinely ordained means to salvation.

Normally, there is no salvation apart from preaching. The preaching of the Word of God is referred to in the *Shorter Catechism* as 'the outward and ordinary means whereby Christ communicateth to us the benefits of redemption' (Q.88). Question 89 of the *Shorter Catechism* asks 'How is the Word made effectual to salvation?' and replies 'The Spirit of God maketh the reading, but especially the preaching of the Word an effectual means of convincing and converting sinners, and of building them up in holiness and comfort, through faith unto salvation.' That this is so is both the testimony of Scripture and the subsequent history of the church. A revival of Biblical Christianity has always gone hand-in-hand with a revival of Biblical preaching. Oh that God would raise up faithful Biblical preachers in our day, and give His people a hunger to hear His Word.

eleven

ThE PlanS

Confident of your obedience, I write to you, knowing that you will do even more than I say. At the same time, prepare a guest room for me, for I am hoping through your prayers to be granted to you (vv.21,22).

PAUL'S PLANS, IN THE WILL OF THE LORD (CF JAMES 4:15), WERE TO VISIT PHILEMON IN COLOSSAE, after he had been released from prison. These plans were actually yet another covert reason for Philemon to receive Onesimus as a Christian brother. How embarrassing for Philemon if Paul should pay him a call and find out that he had disregarded his request! Paul, however, expected the very best from Philemon – *knowing that you will do even more than I say.* Grace is always superabundant and munificent.

We cannot actually say whether Philemon did receive Onesimus back as a brother or not, as we lack the clear evidence either way. But it is unthinkable that he did not. Would this lovely letter have found a place in the inspired Book of God if he had gone against Paul's request? It is most doubtful.

i. Please prepare a guest room for me.

Christian hospitality was seen as a great necessity and virtue in Bible days, when inns were notorious for their unlicensed licentiousness (cf 1 Timothy 3:2, Hebrews 13:2 and 1 Peter 4:9). Countless Christians since - the writer being one of them - can testify their indebtedness to those Christians who open up their homes as well as their hearts to their fellow believers.

ii. Please pray I'll be released to you.

I am hoping through your prayers to be granted to you . . .

Paul opened this little letter by informing Philemon and his friends of his prayers for them (see v.4). Here though he asks for their prayers for him (the 'you' is plural). Paul was one who believed that prayer changes things. It is significant that he brought 1 Thessalonians to an end with the terse *Brethren, pray for us* (1 Thessalonians 5:25).

It is a great and infathomable mystery as to how God's sovereign providence and foreordination of all the details of life are somehow linked to and interwoven with our feeble prayers. Of course, prayer can never change or alter God's eternal decree, as the purpose of prayer is not to get man's will done in heaven, but God's will done here on earth. Somehow though, God has woven our prayers into the fabric of His providence. Paul just would not have said 'What's the point of praying? If God has ordained that I'll be released I'll be released. If He has ordained that I'll stay then I'll stay.' No. Paul, whilst believing in God's providence (cf Ephesians 1:11) also believed in a God Who answers prayer. God is certainly not dependant on our prayers (!), and yet He uses our prayers as a means to accomplish His providential purposes.

To illustrate this, we may muse that perhaps Luke, who was with Paul in prison, had informed Paul about the time when Peter likewise had been in prison. Luke recorded the incident in Acts 12. Prayer there had certainly changed things, and the situation was so similar: *Peter was kept in prison; but earnest prayer for him was made to God by the church* (Acts 12:5). If you know the incident, you will know that God answered those earnest prayers of the church. Peter was released from prison – the unbelief of the church notwithstanding! Verse 16ff. relates how Peter then went and knocked at the house where the believers were staying. *Peter continued knocking; and when they opened, they saw him and were amazed. But motioning them to be silent, he described to them how the Lord had brought him out of prison.*

In application, do we believe in the power of prayer? Better, do we believe in the God Who answers prayer? In the Old Testament, God is referred to as *O Thou who hearest prayer* (Psalm 65:2).

Jesus once *told them a parable to the effect that they ought always to pray and not lose heart* (Luke 18:1). Answered prayer gives us incentive to pray. It is a victorious circle! The psalmist testified *I love the Lord, because He has heard my voice and my supplication. Because He inclined His ear to me, therefore I will call on Him as long as I live* (Psalm

116:1,2). And he penned those verses way before the Son of God walked upon this earth and said to His disciples *Ask and you will receive, that your joy may be full* (John 16:24).

twelve
THE PEERS

*Epaphras, my fellow prisoner in Christ Jesus sends greetings to
you, and so do Mark, Aristarchas, Demas and Luke, my fellow
workers* (vv. 23,24).

ALTHOUGH INCARCERATED IN PRISON, PAUL DID
NOT LACK FOR COMPANIONSHIP. FIVE OF HIS
companions are listed here, and we can be sure that he appreciated their presence with him through his trials, as they
ministered both prayerful and practical support. We can be sure
too that the appreciation was mutual.

When we find ourselves in dire straights, we soon real-
ise who our true friends are, and who are our mere aquaintances.
There are friends who appear to be friends, but there is a friend

who sticks closer than a brother (Proverbs 18:24). The Bible defines a friend like this: *A friend loves at all times and a brother is born for adversity* (Proverbs 17:17). Paul was blessed with friends in adversity. Let us now take a closer look at Paul's friends – a fellow prisoner and fellow workers:-

1. Epaphras, my fellow prisoner in Christ Jesus sends greetings to you . . .

Epaphras's greetings would have immediately stuck a warm chord in the hearts of the church at Philemon's house in Colossae. *Epaphras, who is one of yourselves* (Colossians 4:12). How they loved Ephaphras. He was their fellow countryman. More though, they also loved Epaphras because he was the human instrument and agent through whom had God founded their church. . . . *you have heard before in the word of truth, the gospel which has come to you . . . as you learned it from Epaphras our fellow servant. He is a faithful minister of Christ on your behalf* (Colossians 1:5,7).What a way to go down in history! Epaphras was *a faithful minister of Christ.*

Now though, Epaphras was in prison for his faithfulness to Christ. Even this though could not chain his ministry, as Colossians 4:12 shows that even in prison, Epaphras was a man of intense prayer, and true prayer always has practical effects – it moves mountains! *Epaphras, who is one of yourselves, a servant of Christ Jesus, greets you, always remembering you earnestly in his prayers, that you may stand mature and fully assured in the will of God.* We could do with more of Epaphras's kind today: faithful preachers and fervent pleaders.

2. Mark.

We are indebted to John Mark for his wonderful Gospel.

It is the shortest and tersest of the four, in which He portrays the Lord Jesus as the suffering servant of God. *The Son of Man came not to be served but to serve and to give His life as a ransom for many* (Mark 10:45), reads the clue verse of Mark's Gospel.

Scripture though is candid. It paints a picture of Mark 'warts and all'. On Paul's first missionary journey we are told *Now Paul and his company set sail from Paphos, and came to Perga in Pamphlia. And Mark left them and returned to Jerusalem* (Acts 13:13). Mark's 'cold feet' were such that Paul initially had grave doubts as to his stickability. Mark's instability was the cause of a division between Paul on the one hand and Barnabbas and Mark - who were cousins - on the other. The Bible pulls no punches. It reveals that even born again believers sometimes disagree and fall out. *And Barnabas wanted to take with them John called Mark. But Paul thought best not to take with them one who had withdrawn from them in Pamphylia, and had not gone with them to the work. And there was a sharp contention, so that they separated from each other . . .* (Acts 15:37 ff.).

By the time of this letter to Philemon though, Paul and Mark were back together. Failure need not be final in the Christian life, praise God. There is restorative grace, as Abraham, David, Peter and Mark would all testify. Mark eventually really proved his worth to Paul. In the final letter that Paul wrote – again from prison – he requested to Timothy: *Get Mark and bring him with you; for he is very useful in serving me* (2 Timothy 4:11).

3. Aristarchus.

References to Aristarchus in the Bible are sparse. Acts 19:29 mentions *Gaius and Aristarchus, who were Paul's companions in travel.* In Acts 20:4 we see him accompanying

Paul to Jerusalem, and in Acts 27:2 we see him sailing with Paul to Rome, getting shipwrecked in the process. Here we see him in prison with Paul. All this evidence evidences Aristarchus's friendship and faithfulness to Paul through thick and thin. He was evidently good company and Paul enjoyed and appreciated his being around. If we need a model for what it is to be a friend, Aristarchus is our man.

4. Demas.

In reading of Paul's happy companionship in his adversity, Demas comes as 'the fly in the ointment.' He is described here as one of Paul's 'fellow workers'. It comes as a sad jolt therefore when we read later Paul's report that *Demas, in love with this present world, has deserted me . . .* (2 Timothy 4:10)

Demas began well, but did not last. He acts as a stern warning to us all. Every church seems to know someone who once attended most faithfully, but for various reasons fell away. *Therefore let any one who thinks that he stands take heed lest he fall* (1 Corinthians 1:10).

The temptations of this world proved to be too strong for Demas. Jesus Himself warned that this might happen. . . . *others are the ones sown among thorns; they are those who hear the word, but the cares of the world, and the delight in riches, and the desire for other things enter in and choke the word, and it proves unfruitful* (Mark 4:19). Remember Demas and take heed!

> And if one of Paul's associates became weary and discouraged and was afterwards drawn away by the vanity of the world, let none of us rely too much on our own zeal lasting even one year, but remembering how much of the journey still lies ahead, let us ask God for steadfastness. (John Calvin).

5. *Luke.*

Luke the beloved physician (Colossians 4:14). Paul would have really appreciated Luke's medical care and skill, as he knew what it was to be plagued by ill health – see 2 Corinthians 12:7 ff. – as indeed most of us will this side of eternity. Paul's lifestyle and the very conditions of his prison cell in Rome were hardly conducive to being free from bodily ailments.

Almighty God has His friends, and He has His own way of linking up these friends on earth for their mutual benefit. Such was the case with Luke and Paul. Luke stayed by Paul to the end. Paul was to record in his final letter and imprisonment, just before his death *Luke alone is with me* (2 Timothy 4:11).

Luke, of course, was also a gifted writer and a respected and careful historian, as well as being a medical doctor. We are indebted to him for his carefully researched Gospel (see Luke 1:1-4) in which he portrays Jesus as the compassionate Son of Man Who came to seek and to save the lost (see Luke 19:10). Under the guidance and influence of the Holy Spirit, Luke eventually added another volume to his Gospel – the Acts of the Apostles. In this he records the thrilling story of the spread of the Gospel and the establishment of the church. A fuller title to Acts would perhaps be 'The Acts of the Risen Christ by His Holy Spirit through His Apostles.'

(As a sidelight, we notice that two Gospel writers are here with Paul in prison, namely Mark and Luke. We smile therefore when we hear liberal theologians suggest that Paul knew nothing of the historical Jesus and attempt to drive a wedge between the Jesus of history and the Christ of faith. The Jesus of history is the Christ of faith!)

Paul's peers: Epaphras, Mark, Aristarchus, Demas and Luke. What a variety of men attached themselves to Paul. How varied were their backgrounds, gifts and abilities. Their differences though did not prevent their working and praying together. Such is always the case with the one Church – the body of Christ where each member works and prays for the common good and the glory of God.

thirteen

ThE ParTinG

The grace of the Lord Jesus Christ be with your spirit (v.25).

IN THIS WAY PAUL ENDS THIS GRACIOUS LITTLE
LETTER TO PHILEMON. BEGINNING WITH *GRACE
to you and peace from God our Father and the Lord Jesus
Christ* (v.3) he now closes with *The grace of the Lord Jesus
Christ be with your spirit* .

Paul was saved by grace. Paul was kept by God's grace.
Paul was a preacher of God's grace in Jesus Christ. 'Grace' is
the trademark of all his letters. Paul knew that Philemon too
had been a recipient of God's saving grace in Jesus Christ, and
this letter to Philemon was written with the hope that Philemon

would now show grace to Onesimus – who also had experienced God's saving grace.

> The apostle has asked much. He will end with a greeting which is also a prayer. The Lord Jesus Christ who gave infinitely much to redeem Philemon will give him grace to perform all that has been asked and more! (H. A. Carson).

And so we leave this short note to Philemon – *A Postcard from Paul!* If we are believers we have surely seen ourselves mirrored here. How easy it is to relate to Onesimus, the prodigal slave. We may even be able to recall the exact time when God's grace arrested us when we were wandering far from him. ''Tis grace that brought us safe this far, and grace will lead us home.' All praise to the Triune *God of all grace* (1 Peter 5:10). May God's grace give us a testimony similar to Onesimus. And may God's grace enable us to show the graciousness of Philemon.

> Jesus sought me when a stranger
> Wandering from the fold of God
> He to save my soul from danger
> Interposed His precious blood
>
> Oh to grace how great a debtor
> Daily I'm constrained to be
> Let that grace Lord like a fetter
> Bind my wandering heart to Thee
>
> Prone to wander, Lord I feel it
> Prone to leave the Lord I love
> Here's my heart Lord, take and seal it
> Seal it for Thy courts above.

SOLI DEO GLORIA

NOTES

1. *I hear of your love and . . . faith . . . (v. 5).*

If we wish to know how it was that Paul, a prisoner in Rome, had heard of the love and faith of Philemon - a master in Colossae - we have only to compare Scripture with Scripture:-

The human instrument in founding the church at Colossae was Epaphras: *you have heard . . . the Word of truth, the Gospel . . . as you learned it from Epaphras our beloved fellow servant . . . (and) faithful minister of Christ* (Colossians 1:5 ff.). Although Paul, as yet, had never visited Colossae, when he was writing to Philemon there, in the mystery of providence, Epaphras was now his cell-mate in Rome - *Epaphras, my fellow prisoner in Christ Jesus, sends greetings to you* (v.23).

It was through Epaphras therefore that Paul heard of Philemon's love and faith. As Philemon was, humanly speaking, one of Paul's converts (see vv.19b and 20, most probably during the time of Paul's extended stay in Ephesus), Paul would no doubt have taken a special interest in Epaphras's report of Philemon's progess in the faith.

2. *Though I am bold enough in Christ to command you to do what is required, yet for love's sake I prefer to appeal to you.* (vv.8-9).

These verses reveal Paul's awareness of his apostolic authority - even though he here voluntarily laid it aside. 'Since Paul has been given impressive proof of Philemon's love, he will not invoke his authority as an apostle to command what ought to be done. He prefers to entreat 'for love's sake.' This phrase does not refer to the love of Philemon or Paul, but to 'love absolutely, love regarded as a principle which demands deferential respect' (Lightfoot), (Wilson).

As these verses raise the question of apostolic authority, it may be helpful to remind the reader that an apostle was 'one sent with a commission', i.e. one commissioned by Christ. Paul's authority over the churches lay in the fact that he had been divinely commissioned for his life's work: *Paul - an apostle - not from men nor through man, but through Jesus Christ and God the Father* (Galatians 1:1); *Paul, called by the will of God to be an apostle of Christ Jesus . . .* (1 Corinthians 1:1). Paul therefore exercised a special authority over both individuals and assemblies. He could claim that *it is God Who establishes us with you in Christ, and has commissioned us* (2 Corinthians 1:21).

Whilst the office of an apostle was unique to the first century, believers today are yet under apostolic authority in that they are subject to the apostolic writings as contained in the New Testament Scriptures - the Scriptures being the sole authority for belief and behaviour in both the life of the individual and the life of the assembly. (One could even be as bold as to suggest that when a preacher preaches the Gospel faithfully, he is in some sense exercising apostolic authority).

3. Considering that the main subject of the epistle to Philemon is that of Paul's returning of Onesimus - a renegade but now regenerate and reformed slave - to his master, a careful Bible reader may wonder why Paul, so well versed in the Torah as he was, did not bring Deuteronomy 23:15-16 into the equation:-

You shall not give up to his master a slave who has

escaped from his master to you; he shall dwell with you in your midst . . .

The short answer to this is 'the Gospel'. Onesimus was now *more than a slave, . . . a beloved brother, especially to me but how much more to you* (v.16).

Whilst the Christian aspires to keep the law of God - not to gain salvation, but out of gratitude for a salvation freely given - in certain instances the law of God has been superseded by the Gospel. Such instances would include the sacrificial system of the Old Testament - since fulfilled in the One Sacrifice of Christ at Calvary, the observing of the Sabbath Day on the first, as opposed to the seventh day of the week - due to the resurrection of Christ on that day, and also the case here of a converted slave being returned to his Christian master.

In Paul's returning of Onesimus, we note that whilst it was the Christian faith which was responsible for the abolition of slavery, the apostles were not social reformers per se. They sought not to change institutions, but the hearts of the individuals living within those institutions - a revolution from within rather than from without. From Paul's words in 1 Timothy 6:1,2, we can deduce that Onesimus now had even greater incentive to serve his earthly master well:-

Let all who are under the yoke of slavery regard their masters as worthy of all honour, so that the name of God and the teaching may not be defamed. Those who have believing masters must not be disrespectful on the ground that they are brethren; rather they must serve all the better since those who benefit by their service are believers and beloved.

4. *I am hoping through your prayers to be granted to you . . .* (v. 22).

Scripture is silent as to whether Paul's prayerful desire to visit the saints in Colossae was actually fulfilled. Whilst our instinct might suggest that the Lord would surely have answered the prayers for Paul and the prayers of Paul for this matter, we cannot say so with certainty. The Acts of the Apostles end with Paul in prison at Rome - but that Paul enjoyed a further period of freedom after this, before another imprisonment and his eventual execution/glorification, is assumed by many from words in his last ever recorded epistle:- *At my first defence no one took my part; all deserted me . . . But the Lord stood by me . . . So I was rescued from the lion's mouth* (2 Timothy 4:16, 17).

It has been suggested that the problem of unanswered prayer lies on the surface of verse 22, as elsewhere in Paul's expression of a desire to visit the saints. Seemingly unanswered prayer for good and legitimate requests - e.g. the salvation of a loved one - can be a source of great perplexity to the child of God, and presents a sensitive personal and pastoral problem. The apostle Paul himself however was no stranger to unanswered prayer. In 2 Corinthians 12:7 ff. he relates how *a thorn was given me in the flesh, a messenger of Satan, to harass me . . . Three times I besought the Lord about this, that it should leave me; but He said to me, 'My grace is sufficient for you, for my power is made perfect in weakness.'*
Whilst Scripture and experience teach that the Lord does blessedly answer the prayers of His people, when He appears not to do so, the mature response is to bow to His greater wisdom and omniscience, knowing that He is 'too wise to err, and too good to be unkind'. Faith affirms *Shall not the Judge of all the world do right* (Genesis 18:25) and . . . *let Him do what seems good to Him* (1 Samuel 3:18).

5.   A Chronology of the Epistle to Philemon.

53-57 AD. Paul's third missionary journey. Paul's stay in Ephesus (Acts 19). The conversion of Epaphras and

Philemon. The birth of the Colossian assembly.

61-63 AD. Paul's imprisonment in Rome. Onesimus's conversion. The Phillippian, Colossian and Ephesian epistles and the letter of Paul to Philemon.

63-67 AD Paul's release from prison. The writing of 1 Timothy, Titus and 2 Timothy.

67 AD. Paul's re-arrest, further imprisonment and subsequent death at the hands of Nero: *the time of my departure has come. I have fought the good fight, I have finished the race, I have kept the faith. Henceforth there is laid up for me the crown of righteousness . . .* (2 Timothy 4:6,7 ff.).

BIBLIOGRAPHY

The Greek New Testament (Fourth Revised Edition, United Bible Societies)
The Holy Bible (Revised Standard Version)
The New Bible Commentary Revised (Ed., IVP)
What the Bible Teaches (Ed., John Ritchie)
Colossians and Philemon (H. M. Carson, IVP)
Colossians and Philemon (G. Wilson, Banner of Truth)
Exploring the Scriptures (J. Phillips, Moody Press)
The Bible Exposition Commentary (W. Wiersbe, Victor Books)
The Lion Encyclopaedia of the Bible (Ed., Lion)
The Westminster Confession of Faith
The Shorter Catechism
The Apostle (John Pollock, Lion)

BY THE SAME AUTHOR

WALKING WITH JESUS

Walk where Christ walked, starting with His birth and ending with His ascension into heaven. *Walking with Jesus* describes and considers ten milestones in the life of Jesus. The ten unforgettable chapters of this book were described by one reviewer as 'a devotional classic.'

COMFORT FROM THE BIBLE

In this book Dr. Cross illustrates how to draw comfort from the Scriptures in your darkest days. The references he uses are just what you need for any trial you may encounter. God's Word is the only source we need to lift the veil of depression, the weight of sorrow, or the load of responsibility.

SCENT FROM HEAVEN

Can any fragrance be as sweet as the loveliness of Christ? In this rich, devotional, typological study, the author points out that our blessing derives from Christ's bruising. As fragrant plants do not yield their sweet perfumes unless they are crushed, likewise, if our Saviour had not been crushed at Calvary, He could not have given His sweetest pardon.

MY FATHER'S HOUSE

The glory that awaits the child of God is unspeakable and unimaginable. Beautifully pictured in this book is a small glimpse of what heaven holds for us. After a peek into heaven, you will view your day-to-day tasks in a different light.

A STRING OF PEARLS

In this simple but profound book, the author has mined some of the precious treasures of the Bible for you. Containing a wealth of interest, intrigue and inspiration, an enjoyable, enlightening, edifying and enriching reading experience awaits you.